I0845418
The Roots of Obsession:
Understanding Biological
Factors in OCD
Antoinette Kleinhans

Chapter 1: Introduction to Obsessive-Compulsive Disorder

Overview of OCD

Obsessive-Compulsive Disorder (OCD) is a chronic condition characterized by persistent, intrusive thoughts (obsessions) and repetitive behaviors or mental acts (compulsions) aimed at reducing the anxiety associated with these obsessions. The severity and manifestation of OCD can vary significantly from person to person, often complicating the diagnosis and treatment processes. Understanding the biological factors that underpin OCD is crucial, as these elements provide insight into the disorder's origins and its diverse presentations among individuals.

Research indicates that genetic predisposition plays a significant role in the development of OCD. Studies have shown that individuals with a family history of OCD or related anxiety disorders are at a higher risk of developing the condition themselves. This genetic component is further complicated by gender differences; for instance, OCD is generally reported to be more prevalent in males during childhood, but the prevalence tends to equalize in adulthood. Understanding these biological and gender factors is essential for tailoring effective interventions and support services for those affected by OCD.

Environmental triggers, such as traumatic events or significant life changes, can exacerbate the symptoms of OCD. Stressful situations, such as the loss of a loved one, relationship difficulties, or major transitions, can increase the intensity of obsessive thoughts and compulsive behaviors. Recognizing these environmental influences is vital in developing comprehensive treatment plans that not only address the biological aspects of OCD but also consider the individual's life circumstances and stressors, which can significantly impact symptom severity.

The relationship between OCD and other anxiety disorders is another important aspect to consider. OCD often coexists with conditions such as generalized anxiety disorder, panic disorder, and social anxiety disorder. This overlap can complicate the clinical picture, as individuals may experience a range of symptoms that are interconnected. Understanding this relationship can help mental health professionals provide more accurate diagnoses and effective treatment strategies that address the full spectrum of a patient's anxiety.

Finally, lifestyle factors and stress management play a critical role in the management of OCD symptoms. High levels of stress can exacerbate compulsions and obsessions, making it essential for individuals to adopt healthy coping mechanisms. Regular physical activity, a balanced diet, adequate sleep, and mindfulness practices can serve as protective factors against the worsening of OCD symptoms. By focusing on both biological and lifestyle elements, individuals with OCD can develop a more holistic approach to managing their condition, promoting overall well-being alongside targeted treatment.

Importance of Understanding Biological Factors

Understanding biological factors is crucial in addressing obsessive-compulsive disorder (OCD) because these elements significantly influence the onset and manifestation of the condition. Research indicates that genetic predispositions play a vital role in the development of OCD. Individuals with a family history of OCD or related anxiety disorders are at a higher risk of developing the condition themselves. This genetic link suggests that biological factors such as neurotransmitter imbalances, particularly involving serotonin, may contribute to the symptoms experienced by those with OCD. By recognizing these biological underpinnings, clinicians and patients can better comprehend the complexities of OCD and develop more effective treatment strategies.

Gender differences in the prevalence and symptoms of OCD underscore the importance of understanding biological factors. Studies reveal that while OCD affects both men and women, its manifestation can differ significantly between genders. For instance, men often exhibit earlier onset and may be more likely to display certain types of obsessions and compulsions, such as those related to violence or morality. Women, on the other hand, may experience OCD linked to themes of contamination or checking behaviors. These differences suggest that biological and hormonal factors could influence the expression of OCD symptoms, highlighting the need for gender-sensitive approaches in treatment and research.

Environmental triggers are another critical aspect of understanding OCD. While biological factors provide a foundation for the disorder, external circumstances can exacerbate symptoms. Stressful life events, trauma, and significant changes in environment—such as moving to a new city or experiencing a loss—can trigger the onset of OCD or lead to a worsening of existing symptoms. Understanding these environmental triggers in conjunction with biological factors allows for a more comprehensive view of OCD, informing both prevention and intervention strategies. By addressing both sides, individuals and practitioners can create a more holistic approach to managing the disorder.

The relationship between anxiety disorders and OCD further emphasizes the importance of understanding biological factors. OCD is classified as an anxiety disorder, and many individuals with OCD also experience other anxiety-related conditions. This overlap suggests shared biological mechanisms, such as dysregulation in brain areas that govern anxiety and fear responses. Understanding these connections can aid in developing targeted therapies that address not only OCD but also co-occurring anxiety disorders, thereby improving overall patient outcomes. This interconnectedness highlights the need for a nuanced understanding of how biological factors contribute to a spectrum of anxiety-related disorders.

Stress and lifestyle significantly impact OCD symptoms, revealing the interplay between biological and environmental factors. Chronic stress can exacerbate OCD, leading to an increase in the frequency and intensity of obsessive thoughts and compulsive behaviors. Lifestyle choices, such as diet, exercise, and sleep patterns, also play a role in managing symptoms. By recognizing how stress and lifestyle influence OCD, individuals can adopt healthier habits and coping mechanisms that mitigate the biological vulnerabilities they may possess. This understanding fosters a proactive approach to managing OCD, emphasizing the importance of integrating biological knowledge with lifestyle modifications for effective symptom management.

Chapter 2: Biological Factors Influencing OCD Development

Genetic Predisposition

Genetic predisposition plays a crucial role in the development of obsessive-compulsive disorder (OCD), influencing both the likelihood of its onset and the manifestation of symptoms. Research indicates that individuals with a family history of OCD or related anxiety disorders are at a higher risk of developing the condition themselves. Twin studies further substantiate this connection, revealing that if one identical twin has OCD, the other is significantly more likely to be affected compared to fraternal twins. This suggests a strong hereditary component, highlighting the importance of genetic factors in understanding OCD.

Several specific genes have been implicated in the development of OCD, particularly those associated with neurotransmitter systems such as serotonin and dopamine. Variations in these genes can alter the way neurotransmitters function, potentially leading to the obsessive thoughts and compulsive behaviors characteristic of OCD. Additionally, research into the role of the SLC1A1 gene, which is involved in serotonin transport, has shown promising links to OCD, indicating that genetic factors may influence how individuals process anxiety and stress, which are significant contributors to the disorder.

Gender differences also emerge in the context of genetic predisposition to OCD. Studies suggest that while both males and females can inherit genetic vulnerabilities, the expression of these genetic factors may differ by gender. Males tend to exhibit symptoms earlier in life, often showing more severe forms of the disorder, whereas females may develop OCD later and often present with a broader range of symptoms. This disparity indicates that biological factors, including hormonal influences, may interact with genetic predispositions to shape the clinical presentation of OCD differently across genders.

Environmental triggers can further complicate the relationship between genetic predisposition and OCD. Stressful life events, trauma, and significant changes can act as catalysts that activate underlying genetic vulnerabilities. For instance, individuals with a genetic predisposition may not develop OCD until they encounter such environmental stressors. This interplay emphasizes the importance of considering both biological and environmental factors when assessing and treating OCD, as effective interventions must address both the innate and external influences on the disorder.

The relationship between genetic predisposition and lifestyle factors also warrants attention. Stress management, physical health, and overall lifestyle choices can influence the severity and frequency of OCD symptoms. Individuals with a genetic vulnerability may find that a healthy lifestyle—incorporating regular exercise, proper nutrition, and adequate sleep—can help mitigate some of the symptoms linked to their predisposition. Understanding the biological underpinnings of OCD, alongside environmental and lifestyle factors, provides a more comprehensive picture of the disorder, allowing for targeted strategies to manage and alleviate its impact on individuals' lives.

Neurotransmitter Imbalances

The Roots of Obsession: Understanding Biological Factors in OCD

Neurotransmitter imbalances play a significant role in the development and manifestation of Obsessive-Compulsive Disorder (OCD). Neurotransmitters are chemicals that facilitate communication between nerve cells in the brain, and any disruption in their levels can lead to a range of psychological issues, including anxiety and obsessive-compulsive behaviors. Research has shown that serotonin, dopamine, and glutamate are particularly influential in OCD, impacting mood regulation and anxiety levels. An imbalance in these neurotransmitters can contribute to the obsessive thoughts and compulsive behaviors characteristic of OCD, suggesting that targeting these chemicals may be an effective approach in treatment.

Serotonin is one of the most studied neurotransmitters concerning OCD. It is involved in mood regulation, and low levels of serotonin have been linked to increased anxiety and obsessive thinking. Many effective treatment options for OCD, such as selective serotonin reuptake inhibitors (SSRIs), work by increasing the availability of serotonin in the brain. This suggests that for individuals with OCD, improving serotonin levels may alleviate symptoms and enhance overall functioning. Understanding the role of serotonin highlights the biological underpinnings of OCD and suggests that neurotransmitter regulation is crucial for effective intervention.

Dopamine, another key neurotransmitter, also plays a role in OCD, particularly in relation to reward and reinforcement mechanisms. Dysregulation of dopamine pathways can lead to abnormal behaviors and compulsions, as the brain may misinterpret certain actions as rewarding. This misinterpretation can reinforce obsessive-compulsive behaviors, creating a cycle that is difficult to break. Studies have shown that individuals with OCD may exhibit altered dopamine levels, further supporting the idea that both serotonin and dopamine imbalances contribute to the complexity of the disorder. Understanding these dynamics is essential for developing targeted therapies that address the specific neurotransmitter imbalances in OCD patients.

Gender differences in OCD prevalence and symptoms may also be linked to neurotransmitter imbalances. Research indicates that males and females may experience varying levels of neurotransmitter activity, which can influence the expression of OCD symptoms. For instance, hormonal fluctuations in women, particularly during menstrual cycles, may exacerbate symptoms by affecting neurotransmitter levels. This insight into gender-specific responses to neurotransmitter imbalances underscores the importance of personalized treatment approaches, taking into account individual biological and hormonal profiles in the management of OCD.

Additionally, environmental triggers such as stress and lifestyle factors can further complicate neurotransmitter imbalances in individuals with OCD. High-stress situations can exacerbate anxiety and lead to fluctuations in neurotransmitter levels, worsening OCD symptoms. Lifestyle choices, including diet, exercise, and sleep patterns, can also influence neurotransmitter production and regulation. Understanding the interaction between environmental triggers and biological factors is crucial for a comprehensive approach to OCD treatment. By addressing both neurotransmitter imbalances and the impact of external stressors, individuals with OCD may achieve better symptom management and overall mental health stability.

Brain Structure and Function

The human brain is a complex organ composed of numerous structures that work together to regulate behavior, emotion, and cognition. Understanding the brain's anatomy is crucial in comprehending obsessive-compulsive disorder (OCD) and its biological underpinnings. Key areas involved in OCD include the orbitofrontal cortex, the anterior cingulate cortex, and the basal ganglia. The orbitofrontal cortex is associated with decision-making and reward processing, while the anterior cingulate cortex plays a role in error detection and emotional regulation. The basal ganglia, particularly the striatum, are involved in habit formation and motor control. Dysfunctions in these areas can contribute to the characteristic symptoms of OCD, such as intrusive thoughts and compulsive behaviors.

The Roots of Obsession: Understanding Biological Factors in OCD

Research indicates that there are significant gender differences in the presentation and prevalence of OCD, with studies showing that males often exhibit symptoms earlier in life than females. However, females tend to report more severe symptoms and a higher rate of comorbid anxiety disorders. This disparity may be influenced by biological factors, including hormonal fluctuations and genetic predispositions. For instance, variations in serotonin levels, a neurotransmitter that plays a pivotal role in mood and anxiety regulation, may impact the severity and manifestation of OCD symptoms differently in men and women. Understanding these differences is essential for developing gender-sensitive treatment approaches.

Environmental triggers can significantly exacerbate OCD symptoms, highlighting the interplay between biology and external factors. Stressful life events, such as trauma or significant changes in one's environment, can serve as catalysts for the onset or intensification of OCD. Furthermore, individuals with a genetic predisposition to OCD may find that these environmental stressors trigger their symptoms more readily. This relationship underscores the importance of considering both biological and environmental components when examining the etiology of OCD. Effective treatment strategies must take into account these triggers to help individuals manage their symptoms more effectively.

The relationship between OCD and other anxiety disorders is another critical area of study. Many individuals with OCD also experience generalized anxiety disorder, panic disorder, or social anxiety disorder. This comorbidity suggests a shared biological basis, as both OCD and these anxiety disorders may involve similar neurobiological pathways, particularly those related to serotonin regulation. The overlap in symptoms can complicate diagnosis and treatment, making it essential for healthcare providers to consider a comprehensive approach that addresses both OCD and any coexisting anxiety disorders.

Lifestyle factors and stress levels play a significant role in the severity of OCD symptoms. High levels of chronic stress can exacerbate obsessive-compulsive behaviors, leading to a cycle of increased anxiety and compulsive actions. Additionally, lifestyle choices such as diet, exercise, and sleep can influence brain function and mood regulation. For instance, a lack of physical activity may worsen anxiety symptoms, while a balanced diet rich in omega-3 fatty acids has been linked to improved mental health. Addressing these lifestyle factors can be an important component of a holistic treatment plan for individuals struggling with OCD, emphasizing the need for a multifaceted approach that includes biological, psychological, and environmental considerations.

Chapter 3: Gender Differences in OCD Prevalence and Symptoms

Epidemiology of OCD by Gender

The epidemiology of obsessive-compulsive disorder (OCD) reveals significant differences in prevalence and symptomatology between genders. Research indicates that while OCD affects both men and women, the onset, manifestation, and severity of symptoms often diverge. In general, studies suggest that males tend to exhibit symptoms earlier in life, typically during childhood or adolescence, whereas females usually experience onset in late adolescence or early adulthood. This temporal difference in onset may be attributed to various biological, psychological, and social factors that influence the development of OCD.

Gender differences are also evident in the types of obsessions and compulsions that individuals experience. Men are more likely to exhibit symptoms related to harm and aggression, while women often experience themes related to cleanliness, orderliness, and sexual or religious obsessions. These variations may reflect underlying biological factors, such as hormonal influences and neuroanatomical differences, that can shape how OCD presents itself. Understanding these gender-specific patterns is essential for developing targeted treatment approaches and improving outcomes for individuals suffering from OCD.

Environmental triggers play a crucial role in the exacerbation of OCD symptoms and can differ based on gender. For instance, women may be more susceptible to stressors related to societal expectations, family dynamics, and caregiving roles, which can intensify their OCD-related anxiety. Conversely, men may face pressures related to work and financial stability that can trigger or worsen their symptoms. These environmental factors often interact with biological predispositions, leading to an increased risk of developing or worsening OCD in both genders when faced with significant life stressors.

The relationship between anxiety disorders and OCD further underscores the importance of considering gender differences in the epidemiology of OCD. Both males and females with OCD frequently experience comorbid anxiety disorders, yet the types and prevalence of these comorbidities can vary. For instance, studies have shown that females with OCD are more likely to have co-occurring generalized anxiety disorder or panic disorder, while males may present with social anxiety or specific phobias. This information highlights the need for clinicians to assess and address comorbid conditions, taking into account gender-specific patterns that may inform treatment strategies.

Finally, lifestyle factors such as stress management, social support, and overall well-being can significantly impact the severity of OCD symptoms across genders. While both men and women may experience heightened symptoms in response to stress, the coping mechanisms employed can differ. Women often benefit from strong social networks and emotional support, which can mitigate the impact of stress on their OCD. In contrast, men may engage in avoidance behaviors or suppress their symptoms, leading to a potentially exacerbated condition. Recognizing these lifestyle influences is critical for developing effective intervention strategies that are sensitive to gender differences, ultimately improving the management of OCD.

Variations in Symptoms Between Genders

The Roots of Obsession: Understanding Biological Factors in OCD

Obsessive-Compulsive Disorder (OCD) manifests differently across genders, with variations in symptoms that can significantly impact diagnosis and treatment. Research indicates that while both males and females experience OCD, the nature of their obsessions and compulsions often diverges. For instance, males are more likely to exhibit aggressive or violent obsessions, while females frequently report contamination fears and associated compulsions. This difference in symptomatology may stem from biological, psychological, and social factors that influence how OCD is expressed and experienced by different genders.

The prevalence of OCD also varies between men and women, with studies showing that women generally report higher rates of the disorder. However, it is essential to note that while women may present with more pronounced symptoms, men often experience more severe cases. This disparity may be linked to the types of obsessions and compulsions prevalent in each gender, which can affect the severity and duration of the disorder. Understanding these differences is crucial for developing gender-sensitive treatment approaches that address the unique challenges faced by individuals with OCD.

Environmental triggers play a significant role in exacerbating OCD symptoms, and these triggers can differ by gender. Women may be more susceptible to stressors related to family dynamics, societal expectations, and caregiving responsibilities, which can intensify their OCD symptoms. In contrast, men might face triggers associated with work-related pressures or social stigma surrounding mental health. Recognizing these environmental factors is vital for tailoring therapeutic interventions that consider the specific life experiences and stressors influencing each gender's OCD presentation.

The relationship between OCD and anxiety disorders further highlights gender differences in symptom expression. Women with OCD often present with comorbid anxiety disorders, such as generalized anxiety disorder or social anxiety, which can complicate their experience of OCD. On the other hand, men may exhibit a higher prevalence of co-occurring disorders like substance use disorders, which can mask or complicate the diagnosis of OCD. This interplay between anxiety and OCD necessitates a nuanced understanding of how gender influences the development and maintenance of these conditions.

Stress and lifestyle factors are also significant contributors to the variability of OCD symptoms between genders. Women often report that hormonal fluctuations, particularly related to menstrual cycles or pregnancy, can exacerbate their OCD symptoms. Men, conversely, may experience heightened symptoms during periods of significant life changes, such as job loss or relationship issues. By acknowledging these lifestyle influences, clinicians can adopt a more comprehensive approach to treatment, focusing on both the biological and environmental factors that shape the experience of OCD across genders.

Hormonal Influences

Hormonal influences play a significant role in the development and exacerbation of Obsessive-Compulsive Disorder (OCD). Hormones, which are chemical messengers in the body, can affect brain function and behavior. Fluctuations in hormones, particularly during critical life stages such as puberty, pregnancy, and menopause, can influence the onset and severity of OCD symptoms. Research indicates that hormonal changes may interact with genetic predispositions to heighten the risk of developing OCD, suggesting a complex interplay between biological factors and hormonal activity.

The Roots of Obsession: Understanding Biological Factors in OCD

Gender differences in OCD prevalence and symptoms have been observed, with females often experiencing a higher incidence of the disorder compared to males. Hormonal differences between genders, particularly estrogen and progesterone, are thought to contribute to this discrepancy. Studies indicate that women may be more susceptible to developing OCD during periods of hormonal fluctuation, such as the menstrual cycle or postpartum period. These hormonal shifts can amplify anxiety, which is closely linked to OCD, potentially leading to a higher prevalence and distinct symptom presentations in women.

Environmental triggers can interact with hormonal influences to exacerbate OCD symptoms. Stressful life events, such as trauma or major life changes, can lead to hormonal imbalances that worsen existing OCD symptoms or contribute to the onset of the disorder. For instance, the stress associated with pregnancy or the postpartum period can result in significant hormonal fluctuations, which may trigger or intensify obsessive thoughts and compulsive behaviors. Understanding the relationship between environmental factors and hormonal changes is crucial for addressing the multifaceted nature of OCD.

The relationship between anxiety disorders and OCD further highlights the impact of hormonal influences. Both conditions share common biological underpinnings and can be exacerbated by similar stressors. Hormonal changes can increase anxiety levels, which in turn can fuel OCD symptoms. This connection is particularly evident in individuals with comorbid anxiety disorders, where hormonal fluctuations may lead to heightened anxiety responses that trigger obsessive thinking and compulsive actions. Addressing these interconnected issues is important for effective treatment strategies.

Finally, lifestyle factors such as diet, exercise, and stress management can influence hormonal balance and, consequently, OCD symptoms. Regular physical activity has been shown to help regulate hormones and improve mood, potentially alleviating some OCD symptoms. Additionally, a balanced diet that supports hormonal health may play a role in managing OCD. Recognizing the effects of stress on hormonal levels and OCD symptoms is vital; stress management techniques, such as mindfulness and relaxation exercises, can help mitigate symptoms by promoting hormonal equilibrium. Understanding these dynamics can aid in developing holistic approaches to treat and manage OCD effectively.

Chapter 4: Environmental Triggers That Can Exacerbate OCD

Life Stressors and Transitions

Life stressors and transitions play a pivotal role in the exacerbation and onset of obsessive-compulsive disorder (OCD). Various forms of stress, whether stemming from personal relationships, work pressures, or significant life changes, can significantly influence the severity of OCD symptoms. Research indicates that periods of transition, such as moving to a new city, starting a new job, or experiencing a major loss, can act as catalysts for the emergence of obsessive thoughts and compulsive behaviors. These stressors may alter neurobiological pathways, leading to increased anxiety and the activation of underlying vulnerabilities that predispose individuals to OCD.

Gender differences in the prevalence and expression of OCD also underscore the impact of life stressors. Studies reveal that while OCD affects both genders, women often report higher levels of stress related to interpersonal relationships and societal expectations. In contrast, men may experience stress linked to career pressures and the need to conform to traditional masculine roles. These differing stressors may influence the types of obsessions and compulsions experienced, with women more likely to have contamination obsessions and men more inclined toward symmetry and order obsessions. Understanding these gender-specific experiences is crucial for tailoring effective therapeutic interventions.

The Roots of Obsession: Understanding Biological Factors in OCD

Environmental triggers, including significant life events, can further exacerbate OCD symptoms. Situations such as the birth of a child, a divorce, or the loss of a loved one can introduce new stressors that overwhelm an individual's coping mechanisms. For those already predisposed to OCD, these events may lead to heightened anxiety and compulsive behaviors as a means of managing the resulting uncertainty. Moreover, the presence of stressors in one's environment, such as an unstable home life or high-pressure work situations, can create a feedback loop that intensifies OCD symptoms. Recognizing these environmental influences is essential in understanding the broader context in which OCD develops and manifests.

The relationship between anxiety disorders and OCD is deeply intertwined, with stress playing a key role in this connection. Many individuals with OCD also experience generalized anxiety disorder or specific phobias, illustrating the complex interplay of anxiety and compulsive behaviors. Stressful life transitions can trigger or worsen anxiety symptoms, which may, in turn, aggravate OCD. The cyclical nature of these disorders suggests that addressing life stressors can be an essential component of treatment. Therapeutic approaches that incorporate stress management techniques alongside traditional OCD interventions may offer more comprehensive relief for those affected.

Finally, lifestyle factors, including diet, exercise, and sleep, can also influence how life stressors impact OCD symptoms. A healthy lifestyle can bolster resilience against stress, while poor habits may heighten vulnerability. For instance, lack of sleep can exacerbate anxiety and lead to increased compulsive behaviors, while regular exercise has been shown to mitigate anxiety and improve overall mental health. Understanding the relationship between lifestyle choices and stress management is crucial for individuals with OCD, as it empowers them to take proactive steps to improve their mental well-being amidst life's challenges.

Trauma and Its Impact on OCD

Trauma can significantly influence the development and manifestation of obsessive-compulsive disorder (OCD). Individuals who have experienced traumatic events may develop symptoms of OCD as a means of coping with the anxiety and distress associated with their experiences. The relationship between trauma and OCD is complex, as trauma can serve as both an environmental trigger and a contributing biological factor. Understanding how trauma impacts OCD involves examining the psychological mechanisms at play, as well as the biological predispositions that may make certain individuals more vulnerable to developing OCD after experiencing trauma.

Research indicates that individuals with a history of trauma, such as abuse, accidents, or natural disasters, may exhibit heightened levels of anxiety and intrusive thoughts, both hallmark features of OCD. This can lead to compulsive behaviors as a way to mitigate the anxiety produced by these thoughts. The compulsions, often ritualistic in nature, can provide temporary relief but ultimately reinforce the cycle of obsession and compulsion. Moreover, the emotional aftermath of trauma can exacerbate the intensity and frequency of obsessive thoughts, increasing the overall burden of the disorder.

Gender differences also play a role in how trauma impacts OCD. Studies have shown that women are more likely to experience certain types of trauma, such as interpersonal violence, which can lead to higher rates of OCD in females. In contrast, men may be more prone to developing OCD in response to trauma from accidents or combat. These differences underscore the importance of considering gender when examining the relationship between trauma and OCD, as they influence the types of obsessions and compulsions that manifest following traumatic experiences.

The Roots of Obsession: Understanding Biological Factors in OCD

Environmental triggers, such as stressful life events, can further aggravate OCD symptoms in individuals with a history of trauma. The interplay between these external stressors and the internal psychological landscape shaped by trauma can create a perfect storm for the exacerbation of OCD. For instance, significant life changes, such as moving to a new city or experiencing a relationship breakdown, may trigger obsessive thoughts rooted in past trauma, leading to a resurgence of compulsive behaviors. Thus, maintaining a stable environment can be crucial for individuals at risk of developing or worsening OCD.

Lastly, the relationship between anxiety disorders and OCD is particularly relevant in the context of trauma. Many individuals with a history of trauma may also develop generalized anxiety disorder or post-traumatic stress disorder (PTSD), conditions that share overlapping symptoms with OCD. The presence of these anxiety disorders can complicate the clinical picture, making it essential for practitioners to assess the full scope of an individual's mental health history. Addressing trauma as part of a comprehensive treatment plan for OCD can help in reducing symptoms and improving overall mental well-being. Understanding the multifaceted impact of trauma on OCD is vital for developing effective interventions tailored to individual needs.

The Role of Family Dynamics

Family dynamics play a crucial role in the development and manifestation of obsessive-compulsive disorder (OCD). The interactions and relationships within a family can serve as both a risk factor and a protective factor in the context of OCD. Family members can influence each other's behaviors, emotional responses, and coping mechanisms, which can either exacerbate or alleviate symptoms of OCD. Understanding these dynamics is essential for comprehending how biological factors interact with environmental influences, particularly within the family unit.

Research has shown that children raised in families with high levels of anxiety or perfectionism may be more susceptible to developing OCD. Parents who exhibit obsessive-compulsive traits may unintentionally model these behaviors for their children, who then internalize these patterns as normative. This transmission of anxiety-related behaviors can create an environment where the likelihood of developing OCD increases. Additionally, the presence of an anxious family member can create a cycle of reinforcement, where the anxious behaviors are validated, leading to a greater incidence of OCD symptoms among family members.

Gender differences in OCD prevalence and symptoms can also be influenced by family dynamics. Studies indicate that males may be more likely to exhibit certain compulsions, while females may present with a higher prevalence of obsessions. These differences can be shaped by familial expectations and roles. For instance, if a family holds traditional views on gender roles, it may lead to different expressions of anxiety and compulsive behaviors between male and female children. These dynamics can influence how symptoms manifest and how family members respond to each other's struggles with OCD, further complicating the disorder's course.

Environmental triggers that exacerbate OCD symptoms often stem from familial interactions. High-stress situations, such as familial conflict or changes in family structure, can act as catalysts for OCD symptoms. The stress of navigating complex family relationships can heighten anxiety levels, leading to an increase in compulsive behaviors as individuals attempt to regain a sense of control. Furthermore, family members may unintentionally enable these behaviors by accommodating compulsions, which can perpetuate the cycle of OCD and reinforce its hold on the affected individual.

The relationship between anxiety disorders and OCD is intricately linked to family dynamics as well. Family members who experience anxiety disorders themselves may have difficulty providing the necessary support for a loved one with OCD. This can lead to a lack of understanding and empathy, exacerbating the feelings of isolation and distress for the individual with OCD. Effective communication and support within the family structure are vital for managing symptoms and fostering an environment conducive to recovery. By addressing these dynamics and promoting healthy interactions, families can play a pivotal role in mitigating the impact of OCD and fostering resilience in affected individuals.

Chapter 5: The Relationship Between Anxiety Disorders and OCD

Co-Occurrence of Anxiety Disorders and OCD

The co-occurrence of anxiety disorders and obsessive-compulsive disorder (OCD) is a significant area of study within the field of mental health. Research indicates that individuals with OCD often experience other anxiety disorders, with estimates suggesting that up to 75% of individuals with OCD also meet the criteria for another anxiety disorder at some point in their lives. This overlap can complicate diagnosis and treatment, as the symptoms of anxiety disorders can exacerbate those of OCD, leading to a more severe clinical presentation and challenging management.

Several anxiety disorders commonly co-occur with OCD, including generalized anxiety disorder (GAD), panic disorder, social anxiety disorder, and specific phobias. Each of these conditions shares certain features with OCD, such as heightened levels of anxiety and compulsive behaviors. For instance, individuals with GAD may experience pervasive worry that can trigger obsessive thoughts typical of OCD. Understanding these relationships is crucial for clinicians to create comprehensive treatment plans that address both conditions simultaneously, rather than treating them in isolation.

Gender differences play a notable role in the prevalence and manifestation of both OCD and co-occurring anxiety disorders. Studies have shown that while OCD is more common in males during childhood, the gender distribution tends to equalize in adulthood, particularly in cases involving co-occurring anxiety disorders. Women are more likely to experience certain anxiety disorders, such as panic disorder and social anxiety, which can interact with OCD symptoms differently than in men. This highlights the need for tailored approaches that consider gender-specific factors in diagnosis and treatment.

Environmental triggers can significantly influence the severity and onset of both OCD and anxiety disorders. Stressful life events, such as trauma, loss, or significant changes, can act as catalysts for the emergence of symptoms in predisposed individuals. Furthermore, ongoing stress can exacerbate existing symptoms, creating a vicious cycle that complicates recovery. Identifying and addressing these environmental factors is essential in both therapeutic settings and preventive strategies, as they can provide insights into the triggers that may lead to the deterioration of mental health.

The relationship between stress, lifestyle, and OCD symptoms is intricate and multifaceted. High-stress levels, whether due to personal circumstances or broader societal issues, can lead to an increase in OCD symptoms and the severity of co-occurring anxiety disorders. Lifestyle factors, such as lack of sleep, poor nutrition, and insufficient exercise, can further amplify these symptoms, creating a feedback loop that hinders effective management. Recognizing the interplay of biological factors and lifestyle choices is vital for individuals and clinicians alike, as it underscores the importance of a holistic approach to treatment that addresses not only the psychological aspects of OCD and anxiety but also the biological and environmental factors at play.

Similarities and Differences in Symptoms

The Roots of Obsession: Understanding Biological Factors in OCD

Obsessive-Compulsive Disorder (OCD) manifests through a range of symptoms that can vary significantly from person to person, influenced by various biological, psychological, and environmental factors. While the core features of OCD—obsessions and compulsions—are universally recognized, the specific symptoms can differ based on gender, age, and individual experiences. Understanding these similarities and differences is crucial for clinicians and researchers, as it can guide more tailored approaches to treatment and management.

One notable similarity across individuals with OCD is the presence of intrusive thoughts that provoke significant anxiety. These obsessions often revolve around themes such as contamination, harm, or taboo ideas. Regardless of the specific content of these thoughts, they lead to compulsive behaviors aimed at reducing the anxiety caused by the obsessions. This cycle of obsession and compulsion is a hallmark of the disorder, revealing a common thread that unites those affected by OCD despite the diverse manifestations of their symptoms.

However, significant differences can emerge in the specific types of obsessions and compulsions experienced by individuals. Research indicates that gender may play a role in these variations, with men more likely to report obsessions related to aggression and harm, while women often experience fears related to contamination and cleanliness. These gender differences in symptom expression can influence how the disorder is perceived and treated, underscoring the importance of considering biological and social factors when addressing OCD in diverse populations.

Environmental triggers also contribute to the differences observed in OCD symptoms. Life stressors, traumatic events, or changes in routine can exacerbate existing symptoms or even trigger the onset of the disorder in those predisposed to it. For example, a significant life change, such as a divorce or job loss, may intensify compulsive behaviors or lead to new obsessions. Understanding these environmental influences is essential for developing effective therapeutic strategies that address both the biological underpinnings and the situational contexts of OCD.

The Roots of Obsession: Understanding Biological Factors in OCD

The relationship between OCD and other anxiety disorders further complicates the symptomatology. Many individuals with OCD also experience symptoms of generalized anxiety disorder, social anxiety, or panic disorder. This overlap can lead to a blending of symptoms, making it challenging to distinguish OCD from other anxiety-related conditions. Recognizing this interplay is crucial for accurate diagnosis and treatment, as addressing one disorder may also alleviate symptoms of another. Moreover, lifestyle factors such as stress management, sleep hygiene, and exercise can significantly impact the severity and frequency of OCD symptoms, highlighting the need for a holistic approach to treatment that encompasses both biological and lifestyle considerations.

Treatment Implications

Treatment implications for obsessive-compulsive disorder (OCD) must consider the complex interplay of biological factors, gender differences, environmental triggers, and the individual's overall lifestyle. Understanding these elements can significantly impact the effectiveness of therapeutic interventions. Given that biological predispositions can influence the severity and manifestation of OCD symptoms, treatments may need to be tailored to address these underlying factors. For instance, individuals with a family history of OCD may respond differently to various treatment modalities, necessitating a more personalized approach that considers genetic and neurobiological factors.

Gender differences in the prevalence and symptoms of OCD are crucial to consider when developing treatment plans. Research indicates that while OCD affects both men and women, the nature of symptoms and the age of onset can differ. Men typically exhibit symptoms earlier and may experience more compulsive behaviors, while women often present with obsessions and higher rates of co-occurring anxiety disorders. Recognizing these differences can guide clinicians in selecting appropriate therapies and interventions that resonate with the specific experiences of male and female patients, enhancing engagement and compliance with treatment.

Environmental factors also play a pivotal role in the exacerbation of OCD symptoms. Stressful life events, family dynamics, and exposure to trauma can serve as significant triggers for the onset or worsening of OCD. Treatment approaches that incorporate environmental assessments can help identify these triggers and develop coping strategies. Cognitive-behavioral therapy (CBT), particularly exposure and response prevention (ERP), can be effective in helping patients confront and manage their triggers in a controlled manner. Furthermore, integrating family therapy can provide additional support and education for family members, creating a more conducive environment for recovery.

The relationship between anxiety disorders and OCD is another essential consideration in treatment implications. Many individuals with OCD also grapple with various anxiety disorders, which can complicate the treatment landscape. A comprehensive treatment plan might need to address both OCD and co-occurring anxiety through combined therapeutic approaches, including medication management and psychotherapy. This dual focus can help alleviate symptoms more effectively and improve overall functioning, as untreated anxiety can exacerbate OCD symptoms and hinder progress.

Finally, lifestyle factors such as stress management, sleep quality, and physical health significantly influence OCD symptoms. Incorporating lifestyle modifications into treatment plans can enhance therapeutic outcomes. Stress reduction techniques, such as mindfulness, regular exercise, and sufficient sleep, can contribute to better management of OCD symptoms. Educating patients about the impact of their lifestyle on their mental health empowers them to take an active role in their treatment. By addressing these multifaceted dimensions of OCD, treatment can be more holistic, ultimately leading to improved quality of life for those affected.

Chapter 6: The Effects of Stress and Lifestyle on OCD Symptoms

The Impact of Chronic Stress

Chronic stress is a pervasive issue that can significantly affect mental health, contributing to the development and exacerbation of various psychiatric disorders, including Obsessive-Compulsive Disorder (OCD). When individuals experience prolonged periods of stress, the body remains in a constant state of heightened arousal, leading to an overproduction of stress hormones such as cortisol. This hormonal imbalance can alter brain function and structure, particularly in areas involved in emotional regulation and decision-making, thereby increasing vulnerability to anxiety disorders and OCD. Understanding the biological underpinnings of this relationship is crucial for grasping how chronic stress can influence the development of obsessive-compulsive symptoms.

The impact of chronic stress is not uniform; it can manifest differently across genders. Research has shown that women may be more susceptible to the effects of chronic stress due to hormonal fluctuations and social factors that contribute to their stress levels. This heightened vulnerability can lead to a greater prevalence of OCD and related anxiety disorders among women. Furthermore, the symptoms exhibited may also differ, with women often experiencing more intrusive thoughts and compulsions. This gender disparity highlights the need for tailored approaches to treatment and understanding the biological mechanisms that underlie these differences in response to stress.

Environmental triggers, such as traumatic experiences or significant life changes, can compound the effects of chronic stress and serve as catalysts for the onset of OCD. Individuals who are already experiencing high levels of stress may find that these environmental factors push them into a cycle of obsessive thoughts and compulsive behaviors. For instance, the loss of a job or the death of a loved one can activate deep-seated fears and anxieties, leading to the emergence of OCD symptoms. Recognizing the role of these environmental stressors is essential for developing effective prevention strategies and interventions for those at risk.

The relationship between anxiety disorders and OCD is complex and often intertwined, with chronic stress serving as a common thread that binds them. Individuals with anxiety disorders may experience heightened levels of stress, which can trigger or worsen OCD symptoms. Conversely, those with OCD may also experience significant anxiety related to their obsessions and compulsions, creating a vicious cycle. Understanding this interplay is crucial for mental health professionals as they develop comprehensive treatment plans that address both anxiety and OCD simultaneously, acknowledging the role of stress in perpetuating these conditions.

Lifestyle choices play a significant role in managing stress levels and, consequently, in the severity of OCD symptoms. Engaging in regular physical activity, maintaining a balanced diet, and practicing mindfulness techniques can mitigate the effects of chronic stress and reduce the occurrence of obsessive-compulsive behaviors. Additionally, fostering strong social connections and seeking support can provide necessary coping mechanisms for individuals dealing with high stress. By emphasizing the importance of a healthy lifestyle, individuals can take proactive steps toward managing their stress and improving their overall mental health, thereby potentially alleviating the burden of OCD.

Lifestyle Factors Affecting OCD

Lifestyle factors play a significant role in the manifestation and severity of Obsessive-Compulsive Disorder (OCD). These factors can influence the biological underpinnings of the disorder, exacerbating symptoms and affecting overall well-being. Understanding how lifestyle choices intersect with biological predispositions can provide valuable insights into managing OCD effectively. This exploration includes the impact of physical health, daily routines, and environmental factors on individuals living with OCD.

Physical health is a cornerstone of overall well-being and can significantly influence OCD symptoms. Regular exercise is known to help reduce anxiety and improve mood, which can be particularly beneficial for those with OCD. Conversely, a sedentary lifestyle may contribute to increased anxiety levels and heightened OCD symptoms. Nutrition also plays a crucial role; diets rich in omega-3 fatty acids, whole grains, and antioxidants can support brain health, potentially mitigating some of the biological factors linked to OCD. Therefore, adopting a healthier lifestyle can serve as a complementary approach to more traditional OCD treatments.

Daily routines and habits are integral to managing OCD symptoms. Individuals with OCD often thrive on structure and predictability, which can help alleviate anxiety. However, overly rigid routines can also reinforce compulsive behaviors. Finding a balance is essential; incorporating flexibility into daily life can help prevent the development of maladaptive coping mechanisms. Mindfulness practices, such as meditation or yoga, can enhance self-awareness and promote emotional regulation, ultimately aiding in symptom management. These lifestyle adjustments can empower individuals to regain control over their compulsions and obsessions.

Environmental triggers are another critical aspect of lifestyle factors that can exacerbate OCD symptoms. Stressful environments, whether at home, work, or school, can significantly heighten anxiety levels. For instance, chaotic living situations or demanding work environments may intensify feelings of overwhelm, leading to increased obsessive thoughts and compulsive behaviors. On the other hand, creating a calming, organized space can help mitigate stress and reduce triggers. Awareness of one's surroundings and the potential stressors within them is essential for individuals with OCD, as it allows for proactive management of their environment.

Stress management is pivotal in the context of OCD, given the strong relationship between anxiety disorders and OCD. Chronic stress can lead to a cycle of increased anxiety, which often triggers obsessive thoughts and compulsive behaviors. Incorporating stress-reducing techniques, such as deep breathing exercises, regular physical activity, and adequate sleep, can significantly influence the severity of OCD symptoms. Lifestyle changes that prioritize mental health, such as cultivating supportive relationships and engaging in leisure activities, can also alleviate stress and enhance resilience against OCD. Recognizing the interplay between lifestyle choices and OCD symptoms is crucial for developing effective coping strategies and improving overall quality of life.

Coping Mechanisms and Their Efficacy

Coping mechanisms play a crucial role in managing obsessive-compulsive disorder (OCD), particularly in the context of its biological underpinnings. These mechanisms can be categorized into adaptive and maladaptive strategies. Adaptive coping strategies include problem-solving, seeking social support, and utilizing relaxation techniques, which can help mitigate the intensity of OCD symptoms. Maladaptive strategies, such as avoidance or substance abuse, may provide temporary relief but often exacerbate the disorder in the long term. Understanding the efficacy of these coping mechanisms requires a comprehensive view of how they interact with biological factors, environmental triggers, and individual differences, including gender.

Research indicates that gender differences significantly influence the coping strategies employed by individuals with OCD. Studies show that women may be more likely to engage in social support-seeking behaviors, while men might lean toward problem-solving approaches. These differences may stem from societal expectations and norms about emotional expression and vulnerability. Consequently, the effectiveness of coping mechanisms can vary by gender, highlighting the importance of tailored interventions that consider these differences. Furthermore, the biological factors associated with OCD, such as neurochemical imbalances, can affect an individual's ability to utilize coping strategies effectively, making it essential to adopt an integrative approach.

Environmental triggers also play a pivotal role in the efficacy of coping mechanisms for individuals with OCD. Stressful life events, trauma, and daily pressures can exacerbate symptoms, making it challenging to implement effective coping strategies. For instance, individuals exposed to high levels of stress may resort to maladaptive coping mechanisms as a means of escape, which can inadvertently worsen their condition. Conversely, those who can identify and address their environmental triggers may find that adaptive coping strategies, such as mindfulness or exposure therapy, become more effective in reducing symptom severity. This interplay between coping mechanisms and environmental factors emphasizes the necessity of addressing both aspects in therapeutic settings.

The relationship between anxiety disorders and OCD further complicates the landscape of coping mechanisms. Many individuals with OCD also experience comorbid anxiety disorders, which can influence how they respond to stress and apply coping strategies. For instance, heightened anxiety may lead to an increase in obsessive thoughts and compulsive behaviors, thereby reducing the effectiveness of coping mechanisms aimed at alleviating distress. Effective treatment plans should consider the intertwined nature of these disorders, incorporating strategies that address both OCD symptoms and underlying anxiety. A nuanced understanding of this relationship can enhance the efficacy of interventions and promote more sustainable coping practices.

Finally, lifestyle factors, including stress management and overall health, can significantly impact the efficacy of coping mechanisms in OCD. Regular exercise, a balanced diet, and adequate sleep are foundational components that can improve mental health and resilience against OCD symptoms. Individuals who prioritize these lifestyle factors often find that adaptive coping strategies, such as problem-solving and emotional regulation, become more accessible and effective. In contrast, neglecting these aspects can lead to increased stress and symptom exacerbation. By fostering a holistic approach that incorporates biological, psychological, and lifestyle factors, individuals with OCD can develop more effective coping mechanisms tailored to their unique experiences and challenges.

Chapter 7: Conclusion and Future Directions

Summary of Key Findings

The exploration of obsessive-compulsive disorder (OCD) has revealed several key findings that highlight the complex interplay of biological, psychological, and environmental factors in its development. First and foremost, genetic predispositions play a significant role in the manifestation of OCD. Studies indicate that individuals with a family history of OCD are at a higher risk of developing the disorder, suggesting that specific genetic markers may contribute to its onset. Additionally, neurobiological research has identified abnormalities in brain structures, such as the orbitofrontal cortex and basal ganglia, which are implicated in the regulation of anxiety and compulsive behaviors, reinforcing the notion that OCD has a strong biological basis.

Gender differences present another critical aspect of OCD, with research indicating that prevalence and symptomatology can vary significantly between males and females. While OCD can affect individuals of any gender, studies have shown that males tend to exhibit symptoms at an earlier age, often presenting with more aggressive and intrusive thoughts. Conversely, females are more likely to experience contamination fears and compulsive cleaning behaviors. These differences suggest that hormonal factors and socialization processes may influence the way OCD manifests in different genders, highlighting the importance of considering gender in both diagnosis and treatment.

Environmental triggers also play a pivotal role in exacerbating OCD symptoms. Life stressors, such as trauma, significant life changes, or chronic stress, can act as catalysts for the onset or worsening of OCD. For instance, research has shown that individuals who experience traumatic events or high levels of stress may develop new obsessive-compulsive behaviors or see an escalation in existing symptoms. Understanding these environmental triggers is essential for developing effective interventions that address not only the biological aspects of OCD but also the situational contexts that can intensify the disorder.

The Roots of Obsession: Understanding Biological Factors in OCD

The relationship between anxiety disorders and OCD is another area of significant interest. OCD often coexists with other anxiety disorders, such as generalized anxiety disorder or social anxiety disorder, complicating diagnosis and treatment. The overlap of symptoms can lead to misdiagnosis or underdiagnosis, emphasizing the need for a nuanced understanding of how these disorders interact. Furthermore, shared biological and psychological mechanisms, such as heightened sensitivity to anxiety and maladaptive coping strategies, underscore the importance of a comprehensive approach to treatment that addresses both OCD and comorbid anxiety disorders.

Lastly, lifestyle factors and stress management play crucial roles in the severity and frequency of OCD symptoms. Research has demonstrated that individuals with OCD who engage in regular physical activity, maintain a balanced diet, and practice mindfulness or relaxation techniques often report a reduction in their symptoms. Conversely, high levels of stress and poor lifestyle choices can exacerbate OCD, leading to increased frequency and intensity of compulsive behaviors. This highlights the importance of integrating lifestyle modifications and stress reduction strategies into treatment plans, fostering a holistic approach to managing OCD that considers both biological predispositions and daily living factors.

Implications for Treatment and Research

The implications for treatment and research regarding obsessive-compulsive disorder (OCD) are multifaceted, particularly when considering the biological factors that influence its development. Understanding the genetic and neurobiological underpinnings of OCD can lead to more tailored treatment approaches. For instance, advancements in neuroimaging techniques have provided insights into the brain circuits involved in OCD, particularly in the orbitofrontal cortex, anterior cingulate cortex, and basal ganglia. This knowledge can help in developing targeted therapies, such as deep brain stimulation or transcranial magnetic stimulation, which could be beneficial for individuals who do not respond well to traditional treatments like cognitive-behavioral therapy (CBT) or selective serotonin reuptake inhibitors (SSRIs).

Gender differences in OCD prevalence and symptoms also have significant implications for treatment. Research indicates that while OCD affects individuals across all demographics, the manifestation and severity of symptoms can vary between genders. For instance, women may exhibit more contamination fears, whereas men might present with more aggressive or sexual obsessions. Recognizing these differences can inform clinicians in developing gender-sensitive treatment plans that address specific symptomatology. Furthermore, understanding the impact of hormonal fluctuations on OCD symptoms in women could lead to more effective management strategies during key life stages, such as menstruation, pregnancy, and menopause.

Environmental triggers that exacerbate OCD symptoms must also be considered in both treatment and research. Stressful life events, trauma, and changes in routine can significantly worsen symptoms. As such, incorporating stress management techniques and lifestyle modifications into treatment plans is essential. Mindfulness-based interventions, relaxation techniques, and support groups can offer individuals coping strategies that complement traditional therapies. Future research should focus on identifying specific environmental triggers associated with OCD exacerbation, allowing for the development of preventive measures that could reduce symptom severity during stressful periods.

The relationship between anxiety disorders and OCD presents another important area for exploration. Many individuals with OCD also experience co-occurring anxiety disorders, complicating diagnosis and treatment. Recognizing that OCD may not exist in isolation but rather as part of a broader anxiety spectrum can influence therapeutic approaches. Integrated treatment plans that address both OCD and associated anxiety disorders may improve outcomes for patients. Research should focus on the shared biological and psychological mechanisms underlying these conditions, potentially leading to innovative interventions that target multiple disorders simultaneously.

Lastly, the effects of stress and lifestyle on OCD symptoms highlight the importance of a holistic approach to treatment and research. Chronic stress can exacerbate OCD symptoms, while a healthy lifestyle, including regular exercise, balanced nutrition, and adequate sleep, can mitigate them. Encouraging patients to adopt healthier lifestyles may enhance the effectiveness of traditional treatments. Future studies could investigate the impact of lifestyle modifications on OCD symptomatology and the biological mechanisms that mediate these effects, thereby expanding the understanding of how lifestyle factors can play a critical role in the management of OCD.

The Future of Understanding OCD

The future of understanding obsessive-compulsive disorder (OCD) is poised to evolve significantly as researchers delve deeper into the biological factors influencing its development. Advances in neuroimaging technologies and genetic studies are shedding light on the underlying mechanisms of OCD. These developments reveal that certain brain structures, particularly the orbitofrontal cortex, the anterior cingulate cortex, and the striatum, are involved in the disorder's symptomatology. Exploring these biological foundations enables a more nuanced understanding of how neurochemical imbalances, particularly involving serotonin and dopamine, contribute to the compulsive behaviors and intrusive thoughts characteristic of OCD.

In addition to biological factors, gender differences in the prevalence and manifestation of OCD are becoming increasingly recognized. Research indicates that while OCD affects both men and women, women may experience different symptom profiles, often characterized by more pronounced obsessions related to contamination and harm. This divergence suggests that hormonal fluctuations and socialization processes might play a role in the disorder's expression. As our understanding of these gender-specific differences deepens, treatment approaches can be tailored to address the unique experiences of individuals based on their gender, enhancing the efficacy of therapeutic interventions.

Environmental triggers are another critical area of study in the future of OCD understanding. Life events such as trauma, loss, or significant stress can exacerbate symptoms in susceptible individuals. Identifying these triggers not only aids in comprehending the onset of OCD but also paves the way for preventative strategies. Future research is likely to focus on the interplay between these environmental factors and biological predispositions, leading to a comprehensive model that explains why some people develop OCD in response to specific stressors while others do not. This understanding could inform targeted therapies that address both the psychological and biological components of the disorder.

The relationship between anxiety disorders and OCD is also a key consideration in future research. Many individuals with OCD also experience comorbid anxiety disorders, which complicates diagnosis and treatment. Understanding the shared biological pathways and environmental triggers will be crucial in developing integrated treatment strategies that address both conditions simultaneously. Future studies may explore how anxiety manifests in OCD patients differently than in those with other anxiety disorders, potentially leading to innovative therapeutic approaches tailored to the unique challenges faced by these individuals.

Finally, the effects of stress and lifestyle on OCD symptoms are becoming a focal point for future exploration. Lifestyle factors, including diet, exercise, and sleep, can significantly influence the severity of OCD symptoms. Future research may investigate how modifications in lifestyle can serve as adjunctive treatments, potentially reducing symptom severity and improving overall quality of life. By emphasizing a holistic approach that considers both biological and lifestyle factors, the future of understanding OCD promises to yield more personalized and effective treatment options, ultimately enhancing the lives of those affected by this complex disorder.